Having Fun at the White House

By Marge Kennedy

Children's Press®
An Imprint of Scholastic Inc.
New York Toronto London Auckland Sydney
Mexico City New Delhi Hong Kong
Danbury, Connecticut

These content vocabulary word builders are for grades 1–2.

Subject Consultant: Eli J. Lesser, MA, Director of Education, National Constitution Center, Philadelphia, Pennsylvania

Reading Consultant: Cecilia Minden-Cupp, PhD, Early Literacy Consultant and Author, Chapel Hill, North Carolina

Photographs © 2009: Alamy Images: 20 background, 21 background (PCL), 23 bottom right (UberFoto); AP Images: 2, 17 (Ron Edmonds), 4 bottom right, 14 (Haraz Ghanbari); Corbis Images: 23 top right (Matthew Cavanaugh/epa), 4 top, 8 (Darryl Heikes/Bettmann), 20 foreground top left (Brooks Kraft), 5 top left, 16 (Win McNamee/Reuters); Digital Railroad/ Dennis Brack: 4 bottom left, 10; Courtesy of Gerald R. Ford Presidential Library: 11; Getty Images: 23 bottom left (Manny Ceneta/AFP), 5 bottom right, 6, 21 foreground top left (Ed Clark/Time Life Pictures), 23 top left (Paul J. Richards/AFP); Landov, LLC/Shealah Craighead/The White House/Reuters: back cover, 7; NEWSCOM: 5 bottom left, 12, 20 foreground bottom (Olivier Douliery/ABACAUSA), 1, 13 (John F. Kennedy Library), 19 (Tim Sloan); The Image Works/Mark Reinstein: 21 foreground bottom left; VEER/Flirt Photography: 5 top right, 18; White House Historical Association: cover (Joyce N. Boghosian), 15 (Eric Draper), 9, 21 foreground bottom right (Erik Kvalsvik), 20 foreground top right, 21 foreground top right.

Series Design: Simonsays Design!
Art Direction, Production, and Digital Imaging: Scholastic Classroom Magazines

Library of Congress Cataloging-in-Publication Data

Kennedy, Marge M., 1950-
Having Fun at the White House / Marge Kennedy.
    p. cm. — (Scholastic news nonfiction readers)
Includes bibliographical references and index.
ISBN 13: 978-0-531-21095-6 (lib. bdg.)   ISBN 10: 0-531-21095-2 (lib. bdg.)
ISBN 13: 978-0-531-22432-8 (pbk.)   ISBN 10: 0-531-22432-5 (pbk.)
1. White House (Washington, D.C.)—Juvenile literature. 2. Presidents—United States—Social life and customs—Juvenile literature. 3. Washington (D.C.)—Social life and customs—Juvenile literature. 4. Washington (D.C.)—Buildings, structures, etc.—Juvenile literature. I. Title.   F204.W5K455 2009
975.3—dc22   2008037423

©2009 Scholastic Inc.
All rights reserved. Published in 2009 by Children's Press, an imprint of Scholastic Inc.
Published simultaneously in Canada. Printed in the United States of America.   44
SCHOLASTIC, CHILDREN'S PRESS, and associated logos are trademarks
and/or registered trademarks of Scholastic Inc.
1 2 3 4 5 6 7 8 9 10 R 18 17 16 15 14 13 12 11 10 09

CONTENTS

WORD HUNT

Look for these words as you read. They will be in **bold**.

bowling
(**boh**-ling)

movie theater
(**moo**-vee
thee-uh-tur)

**swimming
pool**
(**swim**-ing pool)

4

Easter egg
(**ee**-stur eg)

fireworks
(**fire**-wurks)

tee ball
(tee bawl)

tennis court
(**ten**-iss kort)

A House for Work and Play

What do you like to do on a rainy day?

If you lived at the White House, you could watch a movie in your own **movie theater**.

movie theater

President Bush's wife, Laura, filled the White House movie theater with guests.

POP CORN

After the movie, you could go **bowling**!

Some Presidents like to bowl. That is why the White House has a bowling alley.

bowling

The bowling alley was added to the White House by President Nixon.

9

There is plenty of outdoor fun at the White House too.

Do you like to swim? You could splash in the **swimming pool**. The pool is behind the White House.

swimming pool

President Ford loved to swim in the White House pool.

That's not all. There is also a **tennis court**. You could hit some tennis balls.

You could even ride a pony! Some Presidents' children have had their own ponies at the White House.

tennis court

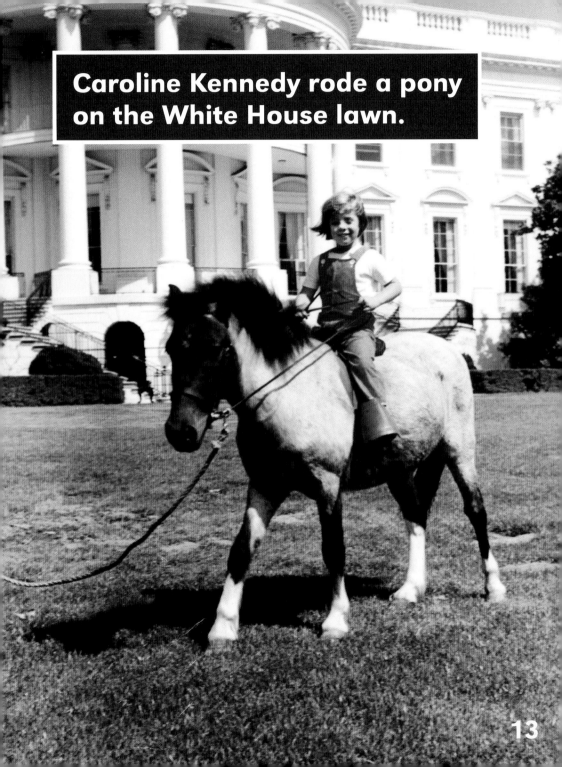

Caroline Kennedy rode a pony on the White House lawn.

You don't have to live at the White House to play there.

Tee ball players started coming to the White House in 2001. Teams play on the lawn. Friends and family cheer, "Good luck!"

tee ball

Tee ball players cheer on their team at the White House.

Kids just like you go to the White House for the **Easter Egg** Roll.

It is a race! Children roll their eggs by pushing them with spoons. Who can roll the egg the fastest?

Easter egg

The Easter Egg Roll is held every year on the day after Easter.

July 4th is America's birthday. **Fireworks** fill the sky above the President's home.

The White House is a great place for our country's birthday party!

fireworks

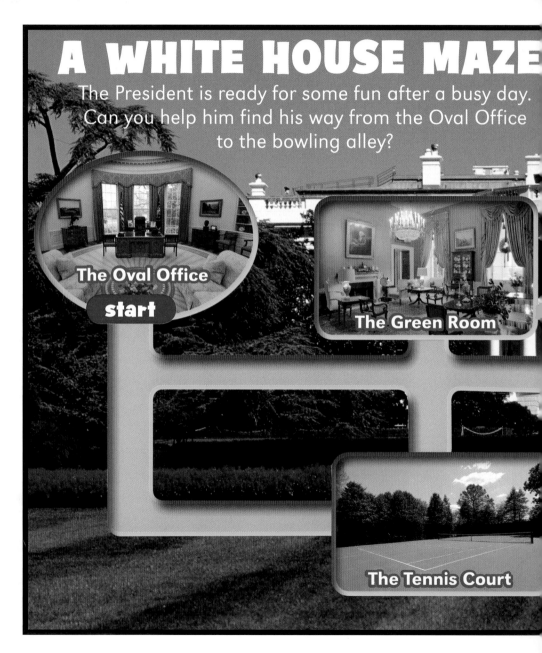

A WHITE HOUSE MAZE

The President is ready for some fun after a busy day. Can you help him find his way from the Oval Office to the bowling alley?

The Oval Office

start

The Green Room

The Tennis Court

The Movie Theater

The Red Room

The Jogging Track

The Bowling Alley

finish

YOUR NEW WORDS

bowling (**boh**-ling) a game played by knocking down pins with a heavy ball

Easter egg (**ee**-stur eg) an egg decorated for the holiday of Easter

fireworks (**fire**-wurks) things that make noise and colorful lights when they are burned

movie theater (**moo**-vee **thee**-uh-tur) a place where movies are shown

swimming pool (**swim**-ing pool) an area filled with water, for swimming

tee ball (tee bawl) a game played by hitting a ball off a post with a bat

tennis court (**ten**-iss kort) a place to play a game of hitting a ball over a net with rackets

HOLIDAY FUN AT THE WHITE HOUSE

Halloween

Thanksgiving

Hanukkah

Christmas

INDEX

FIND OUT MORE

Book:

Karr, Kathleen. *It Happened in the White House: Extraordinary Tales from America's Most Famous Home.* New York: Hyperion, 2000.

Website:

White House Kids Homepage
www.whitehouse.gov/kids

MEET THE AUTHOR

Marge Kennedy has fun doing crossword puzzles.